LIVING A BETTER LIFE

EVERGREEN
INSPIRATIONAL WORDS
Revised Edition

JAMES L. LIPSCOMB

ISBN: 978-1-7320019-6-1 (hc)
ISBN: 978-1-7320019-7-8 (sc)
ISBN: 978-1-7320019-8-5 (e)

Library of Congress Control Number: 2022904334

First Edition: 10/1/19
Revised: 3/01/22

i

To my grandchildren and their progeny. Let this book serve as one of the many guideposts and points of reference in your lives as you learn to live a better life.

TABLE OF CONTENTS

FORWARD

Living a better life is an aspirational goal that should be shared by everyone. The goal may have different dimensions for each person .

This book assumes a shared egalitarian aspiration to live in harmony with others while acknowledging the practical aspects of everyday living – being right is not enough if no one agrees with you. Yet, we often wonder aloud or in silence about what should one do when the odds seem to be against our point of view. For this reason, there ought to be guideposts for navigating the different points of view in life. Life is never as simple as "win" or "lose". Sometimes it means "keep pushing" for your point of view or to "wait and see" if tomorrow brings the answer. Thus, based on decades of experience, the book sets forth some observations as guide posts to achieving the goal of living a better life.

James L. Lipscomb
March 2022

LIVING A BETTER LIFE

Grace and Peace to You,

I am pleased to share with you a few inspirational words that may help you live a better life. I do not have a secret formula or potion. My words are borne of experiences and observations over many decades.

The inspirational words in this book have been shared on social media, speaking forums and in consultations. In many ways they are observations of the obvious and in other ways not so obvious. The purpose of all of them is to better inform the readers about their own lives. There may be a few "aha" as well as "I didn't know that" moments. Then, of course, there are characteristics readers will see in others, but perhaps not readily in themselves.

My hope is for the readers of this book to gain a better understanding of the experiences in their personal lives that will enable them to live, and to help others to live, a better life.

The pictures in this book are intended to be symbolic of the topics of each section of the book. The words remain evergreen in their applicability to daily living.

Enjoy!

James L. Lipscomb

JAMES L. LIPSCOMB

LIVING A BETTER LIFE

ATTITUDE

JAMES L. LIPSCOMB

"Your attitude transcends your actions and lasts in the minds of others beyond your memory of the moment."

"We prefer to keep our opinions to ourselves out of concern that others may disagree. Yet we listen to the opinions of others even though we do not necessarily agree."

JAMES L. LIPSCOMB

"Open your mind and your heart to the ideas and feelings of others to embrace a worldview greater than your own."

"We love the feeling of being "right" and reject the thought that being right may not be relevant if no one agrees with you."

JAMES L. LIPSCOMB

"Whether you see your world as a glass that is full, half full or half empty, remember to also look at the size of the glass. There is more to the world than what you see from your point of view."

* * * * * * * * * * *

"Life is more than the things that make you happy or sad. Life is also being prepared for the unexpected and responding as if it were expected."

JAMES L. LIPSCOMB

"The egalitarian trope that "all lives matter" will remain a part of that tranquilizing drug of gradualism until and unless in hearts and minds of all of the people Black lives also matter."

✱✱✱✱✱✱✱✱✱✱✱

"It seems that as to right and wrong we have entered a time where it matters more or less depending on who did it than as to what was done. Is morality to no longer be a part of our compass?"

JAMES L. LIPSCOMB

"As you walk in the shoes of life, know that every step leaves an impression. Be mindful of others and watch your step."

"A closed mind ignores the lessons of the past and remains oblivious to the transitions to the future. The past cannot be more than a building block of a future that by definition will always be different."

JAMES L. LIPSCOMB

"We can live with water and ignore the fact that we are drowning due to the excesses in our lives. Treat the excesses like water - lower he level, keep your head up and close your mouth."

"It may be easier to see the negative and spiral downward than it is to see the positive and soar above. However, once you soar above the negative, you will live a healthier and happier life."

JAMES L. LIPSCOMB

"Our depth perception is impaired when we see our lives in black and white and ignore the completeness that color brings to our understanding of the world in which we live."

* * * * * * * * * *

"Decisions of the heart are more about how you feel than right or wrong. Know that you can be good and be wrong, but you cannot be evil and be right."

JAMES L. LIPSCOMB

EQUALITY

JAMES L. LIPSCOMB

"We may not know what justice looks like, but let us pray for God's help when we fail to see injustice."

* * * * * * * * * * *

"Moral blindness to acts of terrorism, hate and bigotry is a social value that should find no quarter in the hearts, minds or eyes of a democratic society."

JAMES L. LIPSCOMB

"Our history reminds us that the truths we hold to be self-evident are largely dependent upon the resolve of the people in whose care they reside."

✳ ✳ ✳ ✳ ✳ ✳ ✳ ✳ ✳ ✳

"We were born in the past, we live in the present and we are challenged to imagine and create the future, not for ourselves, but for those that follow us."

JAMES L. LIPSCOMB

"Although created equal, we are not equals, but rather we are as different and varied as the flowers of the field with each having inalienable rights that nurture and preserve our existence."

∗ ∗ ∗ ∗ ∗ ∗ ∗ ∗ ∗ ∗ ∗

"Significant achievements embody a willingness to "see eye to eye" with collaborators even though you may see some things differently."

JAMES L. LIPSCOMB

"Injustice can only be the norm for the unjust. Therefore, do not wait in silence for your turn to experience injustice less you embolden the unjust to hurry to your door."

"Injustice is the product of our enemies and silence in the face of injustice is the product of our friends. Victims of injustice will remember both with equal damnation."

JAMES L. LIPSCOMB

"Silence in the face of hatred, in a democracy that has freedom of speech at its core, transfers the consent of the governed to those least likely to preserve the freedoms of that democracy."

* * * * * * * * * * * * * * *

"The vagaries of life may divide material possessions among humankind, but human rights are indivisible and each human being is entitled to the same human rights irrespective of material possessions."

JAMES L. LIPSCOMB

"Although stations in life and material possessions are not shared equally among people, human rights ought not be forfeited because of such differences."

✴ ✴ ✴ ✴ ✴ ✴ ✴ ✴ ✴ ✴ ✴ ✴ ✴ ✴ ✴ ✴

"Let us strive for a society that believes the respect for human rights serves as the lynch pin for justice for all that should not be attenuated by a knee or rope of injustice."

JAMES L. LIPSCOMB

"As we think about walls as a form of protection, let us begin by walling off injustice, bigotry, racism, and inhumanity in our hearts and minds. The cost will be measured by our respect for fellow human beings and the walls will endure for generations beyond any need for physical barriers among us."

JAMES L. LIPSCOMB

"Justice is not just legislative or judicial determinations on behalf of society. At its core, justice must be those inextricable systemic egalitarian norms born out of the Constitutional promises and aspirations of a free people that serve as the lenses through which everyone in the society sees each other."

JAMES L. LIPSCOMB

"Some say that we are the gatekeepers of a free society. Yet, we struggle with what we mean by a free society and fail to apply our democracy boundaries equally to all within the gate."

JAMES L. LIPSCOMB

LIVING A BETTER LIFE

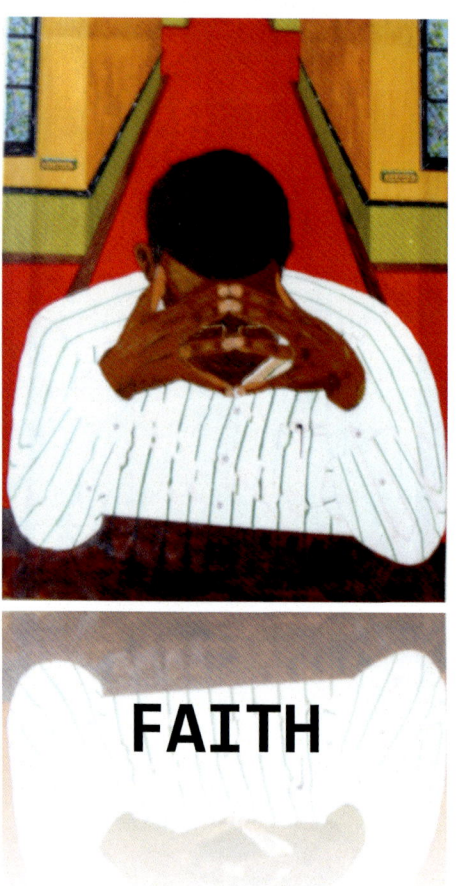

FAITH

JAMES L. LIPSCOMB

20

"I hear "thank you" expressed in so many ways, but my favorite is expressed in prayer - "God bless."

"The differences between love and hate are more complex than we will ever know and yet contained in all of us as constant reminders and challenges as to whom we ought to be as children of God."

JAMES L. LIPSCOMB

"It is not only the Christ-like things you do that make you a Christian, it is also the Christ-like things you struggle with and seek His forgiveness for falling short."

"Righteousness is a relationship with God that transcends right and wrong as we know it and allows us to see things as they ought to be through the eyes of God."

JAMES L. LIPSCOMB

"Are we not all unworthy sinners, blessed by God with a portion of His knowledge, to be shared with the world? "

"When the footprints you used to see at your side are now the only ones you see behind you, know that you are in the arms of God."

"If you open your heart and your mind as you open your eyes, you will see the light of the world."

JAMES L. LIPSCOMB

"Yesterday covers every day of your past and tomorrow covers every day of your future, but today stands alone – arriving in the morning and leaving at night. Will it just add to your past or build on your future?"

"Your future should be less about the life you will have tomorrow and the days that may follow, each being limited to 24 hours, and more about your life thereafter, a life that may be eternal."

JAMES L. LIPSCOMB

"Do not let the words or conduct of anyone take away the peace and joy that you have in your life. Be steadfast in the peace that transcends all understanding and embrace the joy that comes with it."

* * * * * * * * * * * *

"Some people go from "good" to "great" and others go on to be "successful", but few know what it means to live a life of significance at any level."

"There is no greater gift one can give or receive than an act of kindness. Let kindness be your first gift."

JAMES L. LIPSCOMB

FRIENDSHIP

JAMES L. LIPSCOMB

"Do not let the enormity of the misfortune of others deter you from providing the limits of your assistance. Generosity is no less important."

* * * * * * * * * *

"Acquaintances come and go, but friendship endures, residing in the heart and mind while transcending time and circumstances."

"Friendliness is a characteristic of human decency, but friendship requires a kindred spirit that permits one to be called a friend without necessarily having mutual agreement on all points of view."

★ ★ ★ ★ ★ ★ ★ ★ ★ ★ ★

"An invitation to sit at the table is an opportunity for the host, you and the other guests to change your minds about the things each of you think you already know. "

JAMES L. LIPSCOMB

"If you do not know half the things you need to know and have forgotten 90% of what you have learned, be patient with others when they try to tell you something."

* * * * * * * * * *

"We are born to walk upright in all aspects of life and remain above those things that are beneath human dignity."

JAMES L. LIPSCOMB

"An impression is a feeling about you that you will leave with everyone you encounter to share with others."

* * * * * * * * * * * *

"Enduring friendship is a bond strengthened by the transparency of our character and the integrity that lies within."

JAMES L. LIPSCOMB

"Being at a loss for words may not mean the speaker has nothing to say. It may mean that the speaker is rendered speechless by reason of your words or conduct or both."

* * * * * * * * * * *

"You are transparent when others know you as well as you know yourself."

JAMES L. LIPSCOMB

"When you are at a loss for words, know that your presence has already begun the conversation. Your words should underscore, but not undermine your presence."

★ ★ ★ ★ ★ ★ ★ ★ ★ ★

"In lieu of holiday gifts, I would like to see a world that appreciates the gifts of a lifetime - chastity, faithfulness, generosity, gentleness, goodness, joy, kindness, love, modesty, patience, peace, and self-control."

JAMES L. LIPSCOMB

LIVING A BETTER LIFE

"Kindness is a part of our free will, in unlimited supply, that should not be shared sparingly, but rather in abundance. Let your kindness flow as living water to your neighbor."

* * * * * * * * * * *

"We see as much with our minds as with our eyes. For that reason, we may see the same thing differently. If we keep both our minds and our eyes open, we will have a broader view of the world."

JAMES L. LIPSCOMB

34

"Let others take pride in your efforts and avoid the pitfalls of pride in oneself. The former provides inspiration for renewed effort while the latter may inhibit further development."

JAMES L. LIPSCOMB

HAPPINESS

JAMES L. LIPSCOMB

"Your true gifts are shared by you on a daily basis with everyone you encounter. Share them wisely and know that they will have an impact beyond any memory of you as the donor."

* * * * * * * * * * *

"We know that time does not pause. Every moment in our lives marks a time for personal resolution. Let your important resolutions be for all of time."

JAMES L. LIPSCOMB

37

"Your new year can be like pouring old wine in a new bottle or it can be an opportunity for a fresh harvest in an old vessel."

JAMES L. LIPSCOMB

HOPE

JAMES L. LIPSCOMB

"Do not let your ability to do one thing
you like well preclude those things
that you have yet to discover. Life
is always the journey and
rarely the destination."

* * * * * * * * * *

"The Autumn of life continues to look
for Spring, enjoys Summer and rues
the coming of Winter. Yet, it is the best
reflection of the way we have
lived our lives."

JAMES L. LIPSCOMB

"The little things in life add up over time to define who we are now and hope to be in the future. We should avoid or remove those things that would take us to places where we ought not to be now or in the future."

JAMES L. LIPSCOMB

"The hour glass measures time. For my time, I would like to be in the bottom of the glass knowing in my time there is an opportunity in my life for the glass to be half full rather than half empty."

* * * * * * * * * *

"We are reminded that our depths of despair are merely the symptoms and we are challenged to confront the cause and to remove it as if it were a cancer upon our livelihood."

JAMES L. LIPSCOMB

"Joy is the feeling you have when you know that your experiences of good and bad in life are no match for being in the presence of God ."

* * * * * * * * * *

"If life was a piece of cake, I would put love between the layers and as the icing on top. Unfortunately, cake doesn't last long enough in life and the icing seems to be the first to go."

JAMES L. LIPSCOMB

LIVING A BETTER LIFE

KNOWLEDGE

JAMES L. LIPSCOMB

"If you do not know half the things you need to know and have forgotten 90% of what you have learned, be patient with others when they try to tell you something."

* * * * * * * * * * *

"Being educated is not knowing everything, but rather having the capacity to place the things we know in a proper perspective. In this way, we recognize the limits of our understanding and remain open for further education."

JAMES L. LIPSCOMB

"That which seemed to be clear when seen by you may be less clear when you consider the perspective of others. Keep an open mind."

* * * * * * * * * * * *

"We may close our eyes for many reasons, but we should never close our mind from our need to be better informed."

JAMES L. LIPSCOMB

"Be the first to know that you are special and that the onus is on others if they disagree."

✶ ✶ ✶ ✶ ✶ ✶ ✶ ✶ ✶ ✶ ✶

"Our experience provides knowledge that is like daylight upon the dawn and ushers in the risk and reward equation while removing the excuse of not knowing the consequences. Perhaps it is better to be informed by the experience of others?"

JAMES L. LIPSCOMB

"A little bit of knowledge about anything makes one vulnerable to incorrect conclusions that can only be overcome by remaining open to becoming better informed. A cliché is like the cover on a book, not the book itself."

* * * * * * * * * * *

"What you think shows your breadth of knowledge. What you say and do shows your intelligence. Act wisely."

JAMES L. LIPSCOMB

"Because none of us know what we lack in knowledge, we are wise to remain open to the opportunity to learn."

✶ ✶ ✶ ✶ ✶ ✶ ✶ ✶ ✶ ✶ ✶ ✶

"No matter how well educated, how experienced or well-traveled I think I have become, I still find myself in the same place as everyone else in that I do not know what I do not know and I remain open to learning more."

JAMES L. LIPSCOMB

TRUTH

JAMES L. LIPSCOMB

"True beauty, more precious than silver or gold, is not skin deep or in the eye of the beholder, but rather in the character of the individual."

✶ ✶ ✶ ✶ ✶ ✶ ✶ ✶ ✶ ✶ ✶

"Be mindful of your words. Words unspoken can never be held against you. Once uttered, apologies cannot retrieve them, but rather serve to remind everyone of what was said."

JAMES L. LIPSCOMB

"The important decisions about your future are made in your absence. To be present, you must leave your impression in the minds of those in the room"

* * * * * * * * * * * * *

"The difference between being heard or ignored can often be whether you are explaining how the watch is made when the listener only wants to know what time it is."

JAMES L. LIPSCOMB

"Leadership has never been telling people only what they want to hear. It has always been telling people what they ought to know. However, in both cases a true leader is obligated to tell the people the truth."

✶✶✶✶✶✶✶✶✶✶

"If your fence impedes your progress, whose permission do you need to remove it?"

JAMES L. LIPSCOMB

"Advice is very much like medicine in that you cannot take just a part and expect the full result."

* * * * * * * * * * *

"We were born in the past, we live in the present and we are challenged to imagine and create the future, not for ourselves, but for those that follow us."

JAMES L. LIPSCOMB

"When the shadows of the desires of elected representatives stand between the people and their better angels to eclipse the brightness of the angels that stand guard over the people's democracy, the remedy rests in the voices of truth and the outstretched hands of the people to remove the obstructions."

JAMES L. LIPSCOMB

"That which seemed to be clear when seen by you may be less clear when you consider the perspective of others. Keep an open mind."

* * * * * * * * * * *

"Among the options of telling a lie, giving your opinion or telling the truth, the one that you pick to prevail defines who you are as a person. You can always say, "I don't know," if it is indeed the truth. "

JAMES L. LIPSCOMB

"February is Black History month. When the color of your skin is part of the description of your accomplishments, what does that tell you about the history and current state of the society in which you live?"

* * * * * * * * * * *

"The fact that you voted is more important than who or what you voted for or against. Your vote means that you are someone to be recognized by those who need votes. Vote at every opportunity."

JAMES L. LIPSCOMB

"Your unfettered right to vote is the essence of living in a democracy. Safeguarding the right to vote cannot be achieved by processes designed to exclude any part of the electorate."

* * * * * * * * * * *

"Let us remember the true meaning of Christmas by giving thanks to God, our Creator. Let us remember that the blessings of our Creator, given freely and without conditions, are not wrapped or put under a tree, but rather gifted to us from birth. Let us remember that God so loved the world, on a day like Christmas, our true gift was the Creator's son. "

JAMES L. LIPSCOMB

"Right can never be derived from wrong. Wrong is not born of longevity. Like the tides, it too will ebb and be rolled back and replaced with that which is right."

* * * * * * * * * * *

"I cannot carry stones of hate for they are too heavy for me to lift and throw. Alms of love are as light as a feather and have the weight of gold in the hearts and minds of the recipients. It is easier to cast alms of love than throw stones of hate. "

JAMES L. LIPSCOMB

"Like the water that flows in a river, we will never step in the same river water nor ever experience the same day in life twice."

∗ ∗ ∗ ∗ ∗ ∗ ∗ ∗ ∗ ∗ ∗

"Clothing changes our appearance to others. Our attitude determines who we are to others. What others see you wearing will vary from day to day, but the way you make others feel may last their life time."

JAMES L. LIPSCOMB

WISDOM

JAMES L. LIPSCOMB

"The beauty of the earth and all that is within comes in many colors that collectively provides a vitality that cannot be produced by any one color by itself. Yet, we only seem to have clarity, and therefore comfort, when things are deemed to be in black and white."

✶ ✶ ✶ ✶ ✶ ✶ ✶ ✶ ✶ ✶ ✶

"Excellence requires a commitment to unusual achievement."

JAMES L. LIPSCOMB

"You are well-grounded when you do not forget the names of people on whose shoulders you stand."

* * * * * * * * * * *

"The mountains in our lives occupy the pathways to our future. Not every mountain needs to be climbed or pathway followed. Our future is determined by not only the choices we make, but also the effort we chose to exert."

JAMES L. LIPSCOMB

"You can learn from yesterday and plan for tomorrow, but it will be for naught unless you embrace today with all your heart and mind."

* * * * * * * * * * *

"It is not the width of the road that results in our taking the highway to destruction rather than the pathway to life. It is because we fail to yield."

JAMES L. LIPSCOMB

"To travel the shortest distance between two points may mean you need to go in the opposite direction. "

✶✶✶✶✶✶✶✶✶✶✶✶✶✶✶✶✶✶✶

"To obtain the effective benefits of our five senses of perception, namely, hearing, seeing, touching, smelling and tasting requires the use of common sense."

JAMES L. LIPSCOMB

"Tears of joy or sorrow are often momentary but the feeling that causes the tears seems to last forever in mind if not indeed in body."

* * * * * * * * * * *

"It is not only the things you do that make you who you are, it is also the things that you do not do."

JAMES L. LIPSCOMB

"Humility has no race, creed, color or gender, nor name or address, but rather is known only by wisdom for good deeds well done."

* * * * * * * * * * * * *

"Wisdom is knowing that "yes" and "no" are but two of the possible answers to most questions, any one of which may be appropriate depending upon the circumstances."

JAMES L. LIPSCOMB

"A legacy of wisdom, knowledge and moral values cannot be bought or sold, but rather should be embraced and carried forth by others as an inheritance."

* * * * * * * * * * * *

"A little bit of knowledge about anything makes one vulnerable to incorrect conclusions that can only be overcome by remaining open to becoming better informed. A cliché is like the cover on a book, not the book itself."

JAMES L. LIPSCOMB

"There is very little that we will learn tomorrow that we do not know today. Be mindful that the cumulative effect of the incremental knowledge gained with each tomorrow is called our education. Use it wisely."

* * * * * * * * * * * * *

"The only time you can chose your history is in the present. Others in the future will determine whether and to what extent your history will be remembered. Enjoy Black American History month."

JAMES L. LIPSCOMB

"April Fool's Day is not just a time for deception, but rather is a reminder that on any given day things are not always what they seem to be. Stay alert at all times and do not become an April fool on any day."

✶ ✶ ✶ ✶ ✶ ✶ ✶ ✶ ✶ ✶ ✶ ✶ ✶

"Protests are the hallmark of a democracy. Insurrection is the death of a democracy. The difference between the two in a democratic society is when the democracy prevails."

JAMES L. LIPSCOMB

ABOUT THE AUTHOR

James L. Lipscomb is a former executive vice president and general counsel of a Fortune 40 public company. He is a member of the bar in New York, California, federal courts and the US Supreme Court. Throughout his career, Lipscomb held leadership positions in various local, state and national organizations, including the Citizen's Budget Commission of New York, the State Bar of California and the Association of the Bar of the City of New York. Lipscomb, known for his willingness to speak truth to power, has received numerous awards and accolades in recognition of his achievements including being named to *Inside Counsel* Magazine's 2006 list of the top 50 most influential in-house counsel in North America.

In 2004 Lipscomb co-founded the Center of Hope (Haiti), Inc. a Connecticut non-profit corporation for the purpose of developing and operating an orphanage and school in Hinche, Haiti.

JAMES L. LIPSCOMB

The author is donating net sales proceeds of to
Center of Hope (Haiti), Inc.
An IRS Code 501(c) tax-exempt entity

You can help orphans in Haiti.
Go to: www.centerofhope-haiti.org
See also
https://www.facebook.com/CenterofHopeHaiti

YOUR INSPIRATIONAL WORDS

YOUR INSPIRATIONAL WORDS

YOUR INSPIRATIONAL WORDS